True Affections:
Poems from a Small Town

True Affections:
Poems from a Small Town

By
Elizabeth W. Garber

For Dee! Stories & Poems for you. from Maine sent with love + Blessings via Patsy! Elizabeth

The Illuminated Sea Press

Book design by Gretchen Warsen
Cover design by Catlin Barnes, FeniceDesign.com
Front cover painting of "Island Studio Window" by Louise Bourne, (size 19 x 13),
oil pastel on paper 2010
Back cover painting of "Grass and Bold Islands" by Louise Bourne, (size 13 x 36),
oil on canvas 2011

"The Tow Truck Driver's Story" was previously published and read by Garrison
Keillor on The Writer's Almanac on NPR, and printed in The Camden Herald,
Bangor Metro, and Maine Magazine.

"Ode to Sebastian" appeared in another version in the author's *Pierced by the Seasons*.
"Stories from an Island at the Edge of the World" appeared in another version in
the author's *Listening Inside the Dance*.

Address orders and inquiries to:
The Illuminated Sea Press / Elizabeth Garber
79A Main Street
Belfast, Maine 04915

Online orders:
www.elizabethgarberpoetry.com

Library of Congress Cataloging-in-Publication Data

Garber, Elizabeth. True Affections.

ISBN 978-0-9826680-1-6

1. Title

Dedicated
to my children and my mother
who are everything to me

and

to my mid-coast tribe—
the remarkable community we continue to create

Oh, I have made myself a tribe
Out of my true affections

                                         — Stanley Kunitz

One is trying to say everything that can be said for the things
that one loves while there's still time.   —W.S. Merwin

Contents

I.   From a Small Town in Maine

Bay Crossing — January   13
Ode to Sebastian   14
When the Word Goes Out   15
Writing My Mother's Obituary on the Monhegan Island Ferry   17
Ode to Rhubarb   19
Memorial Day   21
The End of Spring   23
Crossing Our Bay of Brilliance   24
After Sailing in the Arms of the Sea   25
The Sleep of Poets   26
Out of the Sky   27
Ratatouille After Midnight   28
Yellow   29
When a Waterfall Comes to Town   30
Ode to Cider   31
These Long Dark Nights   32

II. In Men's Voices: Real and Imagined

The Tow Truck Driver's Story   37
The Man Who Looks Like Elvis   38
Did You Get A Deer?   39
Applesauce   41
The Mayor   42

III. From a Small Island

Island Transport   47
Island Vetch   48
Sea Urchins   49
The Old Spruce   50
In the Summer House Kitchen: Dinner for Artists   51
Stories from an Island at the Edge of the World   53
Inside the Winter Boathouse   56
Island Meadow   57
Where the Beloved Finds Me   58

IV. Of Books and Stones: From a Village in Ohio

A Girl's Fairy Tale   63
Stones 1959   64
Writing My Names Inside of Books   65
Our Mothers   67
Bossy Girl   69
A Private History of Cocks   71
    i. my daddy
    ii. first boyfriend
    iii. father of my children
    iv. my boy
Dancing School   75
His Lips   77
Coins in My Father's Pocket   79
Stones 1994   80
Critique   81
Last Kiss   83
Physics Lesson   85
Stones 2007   88

V. Down East Journey: In Memoriam

Down East Journey: In Memoriam   93

I. From a Small Town in Maine

Bay Crossing — January

Deer dashes across Route One, indigo
dawn, delicate hooves pierce crevices
on ice-clotted shore, quick shiver slip into
Penobscot Bay, arched neck like dancer
swimming into steaming gauze of sea smoke,
aiming for dawn, a ragged tree line burning
like embers, Isleboro, three miles off shore.

Mid-bay the state island ferry rides low, five
cement trucks, loaded and turning, another
summer house foundation. Coffee cups gush
steam like hand-held geysers, fogged pick
ups jammed with crew ready to rake down
the pour. Black labs like galloping seals jolt
a rusted Toyota wagon. Up on passenger
deck, little boy in Superman tee talks non-
stop to mom's ruddy faced new man.

On the bridge they spot something strange
and big. A mess of lobster traps? *No.* A
submerged log? *No.* It's moving. *Deer.*

Churning engine is thrown into reverse
as wash of fur disappears under the bow,
deck shuddering. Ferry rocks, drifting on
torrent of cross currents, waiting. One
bundled traveler watches above decks,
face wrapped in wool, scanning steel
borders. A shout on the bridge. Icy surge
washes deer off to port, floundering, then
circling, neck up, in a storm of slate-gray
spirals, searching for a horizon. Engines jolt
into gear. Last they saw from the bridge,
deer was heading out toward Warren Island.

Ode to Sebastian

How wild to abandon vacuum and errands
to loll under quilts, poetry sated all morning,
hungry for touch. February sun quickens, tight
red buds nub the maples out my window while
beneath the ice carpet, under a frost-aching
earth, I know roots are moving. Over afternoon

tea, the glint in my cousin Kate's 70-year-old eyes
convinces me. She recounts how she rode on dear
Sebastian's saddled back, the first time in 30 years.
"It was just like getting into bed with an old lover."
Her laughter tumbles, dazzling winter's grasp. Roots
deep below flush willow tips into a sheen of yellow.

When the Word Goes Out

Everyone knows it will be one
of these early spring evenings.
Just the right late afternoon light,
the right warmth, the right moment.
Then the word goes out.

Families emerge from their houses.
Traffic stops, commuters step out of cars.
Farmers dash in from outside of town.
They don't want to miss it. The streets fill,
children chase each other waiting to begin.

A circle forms at the center of town. The Mayor
and city councilors stretch out their arms, grasp
hands with shoppers and merchants, cooks and
waitresses, form lines that spread like spokes—
from brick storefronts on Main Street shop-keepers
and artists reach down to the bay at mid-tide, to
elders and movie goers joining hands up High to
Primrose Hill out to the hospital, where nurses and
janitors link hands creating branches of a living tree.

Every year we begin with Wordsworth, "I wandered
lonely as a cloud." As each phrase leaps from voice
to voice, up the hills, down through town, the words
sometime change, rearrange, take on a life of their
own. Along streets of white clapboard houses, words
travel under upsweeps of maples tassling into tiny red
bouquets. On Church Street they "wonder after clouds,"
on Pearl they saw a "heat of golden daffodils."

After the first poem ripples through, a quieting comes.
Everyone stands in the soft light, gazing into early spring
gardens, while birds rustle in leaves unfurling overhead.
Then words begin, murmuring through voices. At first
simple phrases scatter along the voices. From Cedar Street
comes, "Yellow pansies all in a line." From the center
of town, "The first striped tulip at the Gothic." From all
over town ripple the words, "The hostas are rising."

A tension builds. Everyone feels it, but you never know
when it will break. Then suddenly from all over town,
voices, deep and strong, commence a chorus, "Forsythia!
Forsythia! Leaping Forsythia! Glowing Forsythia!" The joy
of forsythia echoes all over town. Everyone grins to each
other, squeezing children's hands, remembering the Forsythia
chant has always been their favorite too, since childhood.

Then words of awe begin to move like a whisper,
a confiding secret spreading out from Franklin Street.
"The rare magnolia opened white blossoms today,"
and "A pink blush at the base of the bud."

Words drift from a bank of crocuses on Congress.
The dusk deepens. "Look into the green at the center
of the daffodil." "Remember, Persephone grasped
the narcissus." Words flutter like a sigh, a balm, out
to the furthest stretches of the lines as evening pales.

From the bay, those who watch at the edge of the sea, send
word, "First sliver of new moon rising." Like a cool breeze
traveling through voices. This is the moment to gently let go
of hands, nod good evening to neighbors, walk home, arm in
arm, children to bed, everyone quieted and filled. Everyone
knowing they will be ready, the next time the word goes out.

Writing My Mom's Obituary
on the Monhegan Island Ferry

"First of all," she says, "I don't want any husbands
in it!" I'm taking dictation from my mom on the back
deck of the passenger ferry, coming home after her 78th
birthday trip to the island. She speaks over the rumble
of diesel engines. Surrounded by backpacks, picnic
baskets, the crew heaves heavy ropes from the dock.
The narrow harbor slips away in a blue dream of May.

I take notes on the back of my packing list. We spell out
her parents and grandparents names, where she was born
and raised. I say, "I can skip the husbands. How about this?
*She completed her education after raising her family of four
children.*" My life flashes by, a brief clause in my mother's.
My sunburned niece calls out, "Don't forget she was Woman
of the Year in the Cincinnati Enquirer."

The late sixties, I was in high school, my parents' marriage
exploding, and she was a ball of fire. Hot summer, the prison
inmates in the 1860's monolith were rioting, banging their pee
buckets on the bars. My daughter asks, "What did you do?"
My mom spells out the details. I add an exciting verb: *She
spearheaded the Citizen's Committee on Justice and Corrections
establishing work release, weekend sentencing, and furlough
programs at the Cincinnati Workhouse.* "Awesome!" my daughter
admires, as we take a break to watch the seagulls whirling above.

I was in college in my mom's cramped apartment after the divorce.
Sitting on my bed in the dining room, she was back from a weekend
in the Ohio State pen, a program she organized to put judges, lawyers,
and probation officers in prison for the weekend. Excitedly she reported,
"I shared a cell with a prostitute and got to ask her, 'So do you enjoy it?'
She said, 'Lady, do you enjoy brushing your teeth? It's a job.'"

In the eighties, she moved to Maine. We skip the next husband, house renovations, the first cold winter learning to heat her house with the wood cookstove, the first desperate job with Sears, cold calls, selling warranties. "That was a downer," my mom laughs. "The best job was driving up to Aroostook County, monitoring heating assistance programs. The poverty there was worse than what I'd seen in city slums. But I'd get a handmade potato basket on my way home." She still uses them to harvest her gardens, freezing everything she needs to get through the winter.

As the mainland comes closer, Chuck laughs, "Don't forget to put in pre-deceased by her 'brother' Chuck!" "But that's not going to be for a long time," we all agree. Pale from the strain of the weekend, in his third year with AIDS, Chuck's been our family's best friend since he was a hippie living in a teepee in our backyard in the seventies. My son adds proudly, "You have to put in that you still go to kick-boxing classes. And when are you going to retire from taking care of old people?" We agree to fill in the blanks later.

We lean against each other, content, quiet. The ferry follows the channel between islands. Feeling timeless, we assume we'll always take this spring journey together, imagining only the children will grow older. The ferry shudders up to the dock in Port Clyde. I jot down last notes. We don't want to forget her homemade bread and pies, how fine she is at splitting wood. My mother's impatient to get off the boat. She's got her garden to plant, now that we've passed the full moon in May and the danger of frost is past.

Ode to Rhubarb

Oh Rhubarb, Spring's tart sourpuss, too often
insulted, soon forgotten, ugly sister to Summer's
tumult of berries: strawberry, raspberry, blueberry and black. Some say, "It's *only* rhubarb."
Even my mother says, "That darn rhubarb, it
moves! Invaded my asparagus patch."

Oh Rhubarb, Spring's volcanic bouquet of
elephantine leaves, we carry you home, ruby
crisp stems to saw into chunks, stew in pots,
bake into pies, pickle, or pour over biscuits
and cream. Grimacing bites before we sweeten
you right, tangle your sour soul with honey,
maple syrup, sugar, apples or strawberries.

Oh Rhubarb, recorded in The Divine Farmer's
Herb-Root Classic 5,000 years ago, ruby-fisted
jewel of kings, more expensive than cinnamon,
saffron and opium, wrapped in dampened cloths,
rocked on a camel's back, as you crossed mountains
and deserts over the Silk Route. Treasures of the East
for kings of Russia, Turkey and Europe: "silks,
satin, musk, rubies, diamonds, pearls, and rhubarb."*

Oh Rhubarb, in England you are cultivated in
forcing sheds in The Rhubarb Triangle (between
Wakefield, Leeds, and Morley), harvested by
candlelight for the sweetest tender stalks, all pink,
no green at all, baked into delicate cakes for tea.

Oh Rhubarb, recorded in ship's log in 1820, you
arrived in Maine and leapt the fence to grow wild
and green streaked. Every year Spring's caravan
delivers you over the mountains and deserts of winter,
and you rise, ruby-knobbed, leaves unfurling, in company
of primrose, lilac, apple blossom, and dandelion. We
carry you home in extravagant bouquets to saw, stew,
sweeten and bake our sour pink feast from the East.

*In 1403-05, Roy Gonzales de Clivijo reported from his embassy, giving a list
of "The best of the merchandise coming to Samarkand from China."

Memorial Day

We pass the percussive march of war-aged veterans
on Main Street as we head out of town to the Little
River farm armed with our binoculars. The moment
the car quiets, we step into bubbling exuberance,
tuxedoed bobolinks swooping the gleaming meadows.

The tenant farmer, in worn khakis, joins us, "I've been
wondering why people keep stopping to look at this field."
　　We smile and point with our binoculars, "It's the bobolinks!
　　Have you ever heard anything happier? They've just arrived
　　from Argentina! Can you imagine, twelve thousand miles?"

He nods, "Today's a good day to see them. I'm mowing
that field tomorrow. It's fast-growing Timothy and I'm
a few days late. See how it's already headed up." He points
out the nodding clusters. "Mowing this early, I get a good
second cutting. I've got thirty head of cattle to feed."

　　Against destiny, my friend and I bargain. "Maybe the bobolinks
　　haven't nested yet?" We watch them balancing on grass stems,
　　before diving into the lilting sea of grasses. Our voices hopeful,
　　"Maybe they haven't laid their eggs yet?"

He shakes his head. "No, they're nested in there.
The adults will fly away, but the nests are in the grass."

"Isn't there any way to slow down and go around the nests?"

His voice patiently explains. "No way to see them."
He adjusts the brim of his cap, surveying the far
edges of the fields. "What's bad is when you hit
a turkey. They won't leave their eggs. You don't
know they are there until the mower goes over them."

He shakes his head. "Thousands of mice out in that field.
I'll get a hundred gulls following the tractor."

We face the lush field, dancing lavender-headed.
My friend says, "There's so much death in Nature."

The farmer looks down, scuffs his boot in the gravel,
"The worst is a fawn. A deer will leave her fawn and
they won't move until their mother comes back."

"Don't they startle and run?"

"No, they don't move."

Quietly, we watch the bobolinks, aerial seamstresses
sewing meadow grasses to pale blue, early summer sky.

The farmer turns to me, clears his throat,
and asks, "Are there less of them this year?"

I say, "I don't know well enough to know.
I just started watching them last summer."

He confides, "What worries me is I've only seen
three honey bees this year. That's all. The grass will
be okay, the wind pollinates it. But without bees, there's
no fruit, no vegetables." He turns, shakes his head,
"I don't know how much longer I'll hang on here."

He slowly strides back along the narrow road, held
in the luxurious blur of meadows, bobolinks soaring.

The End of Spring

A wind is storming through my house.
The back bedroom door swings open,
slams shut, slips open and slams again
and again. The sun shows for moments

before weeks of rain weigh us down and
I am wearied. All over town voluptuous
horse chestnut trees cascaded countless
bouquets of tiny orchids, opened for only

one day of sunlight before a week of rain
dissolved any trace of blossoms. A year's
cycle of growing, the possibility of weeks
of joy vanishes. The trees are littered with
bare awkward stems, knobby and disappointed.

Yet new leaves fatten on rain and heat, grow
thick with song. Even in my dream, in a tiny
stone palace, a bird leans back its head and sings.

Crossing Our Bay of Brilliance

We are this bridge, spanning
what streams ahead and slips after,
as we cross our bay of brilliance.

We are this fresh moment,
pursuing a well-worn path over water,
as we cross our bay of brilliance.

We are the soft summer's breeze,
snuggling through our outstretched arms,
as we cross our bay of brilliance.

We are the mackerel and silvers running,
slipping round cut granite pylons anchored
deep in the bed of our bay of brilliance.

We are the vast wonder of sky,
an ever-changing marvel of clouds,
as we cross our bay of brilliance.

We are the welcome warmth of sun,
glistening on our salt-flecked skin,
as we cross our bay of brilliance.

We are the night sky sparkling
above this glittering necklace of lights
as we cross our bay of brilliance.

We are this bridge for lifetimes,
and for this tiny astounding moment,
as we cross our bay of brilliance.

Composed for the Dedication of the Rebuilt Belfast Footbridge
September 16, 2006

After Sailing in the Arms of the Sea

My bed at home rises and falls as
if I still lay in the arms of the sea.
That great breathing lifts me before
the sigh of waves settles me into sleep.

Eyes closed, I remember mornings in
my bunk, blue square of sky sailing
over the open hatch, awakening to
my sailor's bittersweet coffee kiss.

My hands remember the grip on lines,
drawing in the jib, raising the halyard.
My raised hand feels for wind's direction,
my finger firm on chart as I hold the tiller.

All the while the vessel held us, hull of cedar
over oak. The prow carved an opening as we
moved through the sea, like two hands cupped,
fingertips touching, making an offering, a prayer.

The Sleep of Poets

All week we slept the sleep of poets. Some nights
we'd climb into our berths, like an old Pullman car
pulled out of the station, traveling down this long
valley, gently rocking us all night. Other nights we

were horses breathing in our line of stalls, some
standing, quietly taking in mouthfuls of summer's
meadow hay, chewing with our big well-worn teeth,
in the dark barn. Last night I slept the sleep of mothers

knowing I am coming home, waking as mothers do
to the light step in the hall, the restless sleepers. In
my dream, the poets meet at breakfast to read our last
poems before leaving. Someone brings the head of their

favorite dog, love still gazing from his upturned silky face.
I hold his head, the shape and weight of a heavy heart, before
putting it down, as a paperweight on a stack of poems. Then
a still living dog takes that massive head to gnaw in the corner.

With gratitude to the inspiration of The Frost Place

Out of the Sky

She told me, they were paddling up north, looking
toward the sun, confused. *Had someone dumped*
two huge garbage bags out of a plane? Black razor-
cut silhouettes whirled and twisted, became wings,
enormous, gigantic pinwheels end over hurtling end,
joined at the center with white heads and white claws
grasping, until they gasped, *Oh my god, these are bald*
eagles, mating.

       But I couldn't see the eagles, it was
garbage bags dropped out of planes that held me in claw,
as I was hurtled back to stories I heard in Argentina,
of the late seventies, when students, teachers, protesters
were drugged, heaped into planes, *los Desaparecidos,*
the Disappeared. I imagine the rumble of large bellied
transport planes on take off, struggling for altitude before
heading out to sea. Far enough out they opened hatches
to the wind, soldiers slinging each limp sprawled body
into nothing.

       I imagine students, drugged asleep,
alive, falling, worn clothes flapping, tortured fathers
with spectacles falling, tire beaten electric shocked,
bare backs, arms fingering updrafts, young mothers
held captive until birthing, falling, womb still open,
still bleeding, babies stolen for families of generals,
gray-braided grandmothers rippling in black skirts, all
falling, a flock of angels shot down, wings useless,
spiraling drafts of broken feathers, before they careen,
plunge, crumple into blind water, still falling, a last
slow dance, necks arching back, their lovely hair rising
as they descend into the disintegrating arms of the sea.

Ratatouille After Midnight

In the dense limb-languorous, tangled pull of sleep,
our dream-furred bodies slowly waken, becoming
the Mediterranean-spiced ratatouille we thickened
and stirred for dinner. Our deep green, olive-oiled lips,

tarragon sweetened, grasp on, sucking the softened red flesh
of peppers grilled and fire blackened. Our sautéed zucchini tongues
garlic swoon, lick dive soar in simmering surrender of glamorous
tomatoes, pale moons of onions, laced with fresh ripped oregano.

I bite tangy nuggetted surprise of caper as your fingers stroke
twist the taut bulb of nipple electric, tantalizing, awakening tiny
flames, breath quickening, simmer thickening, rippling through
lissome limbs as marinated ripe olives tangle with glossy eggplant.

Our long simmer dissolves artichoke thorns, leaving our hearts
softened, lemon-stroked, ready to devour, bite by succulent bite.

Yellow

(After my last child left home)

Between weed-tangled
railroad tracks and storage

sheds threaded with vines,
in a narrow corridor of

sunlight, I wander outside
the weight of gravity until

I'm caught, lifted by
iridescent fluttering wings,

a twirling column of yellow,
two butterflies, delicate as

light scattering, twisting
round each other, spirited

like weightless puppies
wrestling in the grass of

air. Yellow wings levitate,
wave, spiral around me,

slipping, riding sunlight,
whirlwind of yellow, black-

edged swallowtails, a free
fall winged jig of exuberance.

Then they soar apart, one
to the roof, the other toward

the harbor, leaving me
standing in emptied air.

When a Waterfall Comes to Town

Do you remember waiting in a parking lot so
long that you started leafing through the Maine
Gazetteer? After you found the page where you
live, where old boyfriends once lived, the fastest
way to Waterville by back roads, you discover lists
of things: highest mountains, longest rivers, all the
lighthouses, and best of all, the waterfalls of Maine.

Some people plan to knock through that list in a season.
Others entice their kids to find the crashing, foaming
Moxie Falls. Some dream of clambering up and over
the rooted trails following the falls at Gulf Hagas,
determined they'll finally get there this summer.
I collect waterfalls off the list, in stories people tell
of where to swim on hot days, how to find the path to
Monroe Falls where eels tickle your legs as you swim.

Once, hiking a stream in winter, I found a tiny fall
forming a perfect whirling circle of ice in the stream.
Some falls become legendary. I explored The Falls at
The Kingdom (terrific tumble of glacier-spilled boulders
carved with streams) at my easel, silent absorption in oil,
painting the dark still pool at the center.

So what does it take to move a waterfall into town?
What does it mean for a waterfall to pick up her skirts,
gather her swirling pools, pack up her bounding streams,
and slide her cascading waves into a moving van? Can't
you hear her? Listen, she's coming down the stairs, swirling
round the corners, slipping under studio doors. This waterfall
undulates down walls, catapults into sculptures, fans across
rooftops, pours in a Niagara fantasy of color. This waterfall
leaps unawares into the dreams of our town sleeping around
her, priming us all with her startling waters, so we may fall
inexplicably into canvases of our own making.

Composed for the Opening of The Waterfall Arts Center
Belfast, Maine, September 2006

Ode to Cider

Grace from the start when blossoms open one
sun-drenched day, the only break from Spring's
relentless deluge of rain. Bees leap into scalloped
furred basins rummaging for gold. Long gentle
summer of sun-bleached denim skies, brief nights
of comfort before dawn drying breeze. Grasshoppers
sing through golden afternoons. Each apple claims a
destiny: burnished Rome, North West Greening, blood-
red crab, peach-streaked Tamanga, purple Black Oxford.

Leisurely fall, frost forgets to arrive, leaves yellow.
Orchard teems red: burgundy, ruby, crimson, where
long ago the farmers wed and danced. One Beacon
alone produces thirty bushels, early bite of white flesh.
Quickening frosts intensify sweetness. Family and tribe
gather, scour branches and grassy floor, cold hands,
cheeks burn scarlet, wooden crates fill: Hudson's Golden
Glen, honey-centered Lightning, reliable Baldwin, sour
Starks. In the belly of the barn a blur of cousins hoist
bushels. Blond beards and copper braids glint under
dangling lights. Apples rumble, pour, grind, dump, tuck
into heavy cloth, wooden grates stack higher until the
crushing wheel concentrates the work of bees, the history
of a summer, into a chilled river of Autumn brocade.

So, raise your cup to the farmers. Sip their signature of love!

For Teltane Farm 2005 Vintage

These Long Dark Nights

a storm is coming
and I hear the far-off fields say things
I can't bear without a friend   —Rainer Maria Rilke

I can't let go of the day yet, can't turn off the screen,
the phone, put down the book, the notebook, lay down
the pen, too many lights are blinking at me. What has
happened to my life? The long slow river of time has
shattered into fragments. The flashing light on my phone
delivers petitions on Senate votes tomorrow, secret
committee votes tomorrow, petitions against arctic oil
spills, voter redistricting, incarceration anywhere, any
time, and I can't go to sleep yet.

I'm swaddled in blankets on the couch. The house is dark
and cold, no, not really cold yet, the winter has not gotten
cold, yet. Some of us have begun praying for snow, a storm,
a blizzard, even icy nights, because we can't bear imagining
what will happen if winter stops coming. The house is dark
and cold and I can't go to sleep yet.

I'm not ready to turn off the light, I want a little more.
I'm still hungry, but not hungry. Not for a cup of tea or
the comfort of cinnamon toast, butter melting into honey.
I'm filled with yearning for more contact, more depth,
more connection before I let go of the day. I need to nourish
myself well enough to go to sleep. Do I read a new poem
by W.S. Merwin, an article on Occupy Boston or permafrost
melting. Until something empty is fed, I can't go to sleep.

For years I fell asleep reading aloud to my children, their
sharp little elbows, ready to nudge me awake, Read Mommy
Read, stay awake for the island where the wild things gnash
their terrible teeth, for the dark is rising, Mordor is growing
stronger, Lord Voldemort is returning, the Dementors are
coming closer, can't you feel it, the cold chill eating our joy,
and do you wonder, will I ever find my way home the way I
once found home, and when, I ask you, will I fall asleep?

I'm afraid for our children living in a time of scatter. Press
screen to connect   press click delete   texted   into
fragments. Can anyone love another in a world   scattered?
The solitude that used to be our own   pierced and shattered.
Are we whole enough   still to love?   Messages
 interrupt   command   You   have to   experience
every calamity   how can you   not know
    melting of   Greenland   ice caps   you can't
         stop   reading   click and   read
click   and   read   and read   until you have to stop
click   delete   click   delete   delete
    but am I   flinging   my   self   into pieces   of no?

I can't go gentle into this long winter's night, hungry, empty,
disturbed. Oceans are rising. The conversations we do not have.
I'm longing for searing cold, cold deep enough to burn away insects
clinging to forests of hemlock, cold deep enough to freeze the ticks
crawling so thickly, moose are tumbling to their knees, collapsing
in soft muddied forests. December and mosquito flies in the door
to land on my laptop screen. Dandelions flower in the yard.

I draw myself to the rituals of night, brush teeth, sit on cushion,
light candle, pull on a long shawl, *om tara tutare ture swaha*,
slipslide fingers over rose quartz beads hand knotted 108 times,
until no thinking saturates me, an emptied mind lays my self down
to sleep on chilled sheets. I curl under a nest of down, my feet
burrow into hand-knit socks, in the solace of these long dark nights.

Composed for a Winter Solstice Community Celebration 2011

II. In Men's Voices: Real and Imagined

I have walked through many lives,
Some of them my own   —Stanley Kunitz

The Tow Truck Driver's Story

You meet all kinds of people in this work.
You have to be polite, twenty-four hours
a day. It was a brutal winter night.
I'd worked since four a.m., finally coming in
to sleep when the phone rang, a guy calling
from up on Appleton Ridge, saying
he needs a jump. I asked, "Can't it wait?
There's still snow on the roads, the plows aren't
all through. It'll take me three hours at least
to get there with the roads like this." "Okay,"
he said, "I'll wait." I went to bed an hour
before he called, "It's an emergency."
The storm had eased as I headed out,
but the wind had been so bad, I had
to stop and climb over drifts to knock
snow off signs to see where to go,
a hard dark climb up to Appleton Ridge.
Over three hours to get to a lonely
country farmhouse, light glowing brightly.
Then a man in, I kid you not, a red
satin smoking jacket comes out and waves.
I think he's waving to me, and wave back,
but it's a garage opener and out of the dark
a door rises, lit like a museum,
a car, glittering white and chrome beauty,
it was a 1954 Mercedes.
A Gull-Wing. You ever heard of them?
I think they only made ten of them.
Its doors lift up like a gull in flight.
I bet it was worth a million dollars.
I ask, "Are you going to take that out?"
"Oh, no, we just got back from Jamaica
I want a jump to make sure it's ok."
It starts like a dream, purrs dangerously.
"Oh good," he says and walks away, waving
his arm to close the door, never saying
a word. Left me standing there in the snow.

The Man Who Looks Like Elvis

No one remembers when the man with the pomade-
combed crescendo of jet black hair first appeared,
but we all quietly pay attention to him. Two summers
ago a guitar was strapped over his back when we eyed
him wandering miles along Route 1. Last year, when
his hair was bleached reddish blond, we wondered to
ourselves if he'd given up on Elvis. This spring, his hair
was black again. All over town, we nodded the same nod:
Elvis is back. Passing him on High Street we notice his
carefully shaved long sideburns, before our gaze skirts
off to study the bike shop window. He's leaving the
supermarket as we arrive. A strange discomfort twists
our faces away. Opening night of *Hairspray*, in the art
deco neon glow of the movie theater, the crowd is thick
with bleached blond beehive contestants, sculpted hair
rising like curvaceous mounds of soft ice cream. Elvis
appears with his blunt heavy brows, the rough carved
mouth, the deep plowed wrinkles under his eternal
pompadour. In the competition for the biggest, tallest
hair, we cheer for rhinestone glasses, pedal pushers,
bobby socks. Later, when we chat and smile, trying to
hide the searching hunger of our loneliness, he slips
through the forest of lacquered ratted hair, a silent king
passing among us, searching for his subjects, his
promised land, a place where he, too, will be recognized.

Did You Get A Deer?

It depends what you
mean. I had nine deer.
They came out to graze,
just feet away from me.

I'd thought I'd stock up
on venison for the winter.
I made a simple blind. I'm
almost embarrassed to tell

how basic it was. I pulled
my truck down in the lower
meadow, a bale of hay to sit
on, a snow fence to hide behind.

I went down around four to wait.
I stayed there two hours, absolutely
still. I had to cough, and fought it,
until tears came. And I waited.

Nine does came out to graze.
Just feet away from me, lowered
heads nuzzled last apples in the
grass. Breathing rippled under

their fur. I held my breath. Two
bucks thrashed in the woods.
Does gracefully reached for
another mouthful. It got darker.

I heard their faint rustling
in meadow grasses. I didn't
move. Didn't want to startle
them. November dew was heavy.

I got chilled through but didn't
move, until any trace or sound
vanished from the meadow.
Stiff and achy, I walked back

to the waiting house, put my gun
away in the hall closet until next
year. I warmed my hands over
birch logs crackling on a bed

of coals, still hearing hoarse
whispers of their breathing,
delicate hooves stepping
further in the dark forest

Applesauce

The State Trooper pulls in as I finish making
the last batch of applesauce. He says, *The D.A.
is nearly ready to make an arrest. I want to ask
you a few last questions.* I know him. We'd seen
each other many times when I was volunteer medic
on ambulance calls. But now an old mistake has
caught up with me and he calls me *Sir,* as we stand
on different sides of my kitchen. I say, *I can't say
anything without my lawyer.* I watch his red taillights
disappear down the gravel road toward town as I step
out on the back porch to dump the bowl of apple skins.
Our fragile old cat hesitates, purring on the top step.

> My bare feet know the damp packed moss trail to the
> compost bin. The stars are so much sharper these first
> crisp nights, the Milky Way's soft blur washing across
> this narrow meadow of sky. That's when I hear them,
> passing above me, first a few scattered zeeps, lilts, then
> their flight calls come faster, like the beginning of rain
> pelting a still lake, each sending out ripples. I focus my
> eyes, wanting to see their tiny silhouettes passing across
> the stars. I pick out their feathered voices, wood thrushes'
> jeen, jeen, seet and buzz of warblers, clear pwui of a scarlet
> tanager. I start counting, one call every one to four seconds.
> I do the math in my head, this works out to fifteen to sixty
> birds per minute, or between nine hundred to thirty six
> hundred songbirds per hour, a great river of birds passing over
> our clearing, while I stand here, the bowl warm in my hands.

If only I hadn't taken what wasn't mine, secreting away
what I took as if it would make me whole or make things
right. I listen for my wife's return, her car's familiar
crunch up the drive, her quick little steps across the porch.
I wait to take her small trembling body into my arms and
hold her all night, whispering, *I'm so sorry for all of this.*

The Mayor

Hey, you wanna cup of coffee? You know, I've lived the last thirty years in spittin' distance of this traffic light in the center of town. I just never wanted to leave. Mind you, it was different thirty years back. Remember the café I ran? I was standing at the bar, when we heard the police chief was on his way down after some underage drinkers. I said, "I can solve that." I just took their drinks. But Roberta said, "No way!" She was six-foot-five, two hundred and seventy pounds. A big girl for sixteen. Worked down at the chicken plant. By the time we got to the door, she and the chief were in a big bear hug rolling down the middle of Main Street. Then they were up, punching and fighting a half hour more under the traffic light. You really gotta love this town.

Were you here when the high school kids stole a car, came round the corner too fast and flipped it under the traffic light? That was something to see! Back then, I was a photographer. Respected artists said I had a good eye, framed things well, but you know, there are a million photographers out there and I was walking around the world, looking at it through my lens. I decided I wanted to be in the world. I put my camera away. Who would of thought I'd end up mayor?

People don't want a smaller-than-life mayor. It's a part you play. I look at it theatrically, cinematically. I read a lot of history. I saw an old photograph of a little town in Latvia about the size of our town, where they'd rounded up the Jews. They were standing in a garage, like Duval's, up the street. The Nazis invited the villagers, gave them metal pipes, caught them all in this photograph before they beat the Jews to death.

You know, in every small town, there's an ugly side, even in this little nirvana, it can all shift on its axis. Remember when the war started? The antiwar people were beating drums and chanting on those two corners, and the pro-war people were yelling and shaking signs across the street. In the middle, the police chief was trying to keep order. His son was in the first shipment of troops over to Iraq. I went from one corner to the next, talked to every group to calm them down. The cops were at their best that day. Our town was at its best.

But the big meetings lately, I don't see you there, do I? Those are something else. It's the crowd mentality. It's which mob has the majority. Poor guy living out in a trailer in Swanville, of course he's intimidated by people with wealth and education up at the podium, the mob ready to hiss against anyone who doesn't agree with them. After four hours of people going at each other I have to go down to Rollie's and bum a cigarette.

You can be the greatest guy but the crowd is always looking for a man to take down. I'm prudent. In eight years as Mayor, I didn't get caught in the bear trap, but we all could. You never know when the mob is going to take you out. Some people think the Mayor doesn't really do anything, just cuts ribbons, but you stand at the center of converging needs. It all comes down to one person, the Mayor. You want another cup? I better switch to decaf. The longer you live here, you hear everybody's story. Someone's kid is sick, or they've got a new job. I hear all the stories. After thirty years, little kids I knew are grandparents now. But you know what the hardest time is going to be? The next twenty years. We're going to start going to so many funerals. When you know everybody, you'll see them all go, or they'll see you go. It's the down side of living in a small town. But really, that's the beauty of being here. That's what I wanted.

For Michael Hurley

III. From a Small Island

Poems written over several summers
on Great Spruce Head Island, Penobscot Bay.
With gratitude to the Porter family.

Island Transport

Just off the long granite-bermed dock,
the weary wheelbarrows wait, under
birch shade in feathery grasses, painted
forest green and indigo. They are beamy,
like oxen flicking their tails, ready
to haul with hand-hewn oak handles,
hammered leg braces, and oiled axle.

Hours after summer people propel them,
loaded and wobbly, across the island,
the herd settles outside the Big House.
The wheelbarrows are painted sky blue,
aqua, salmon, like cheerful aprons with
roomy pockets. Wide-hipped, they linger
like chatting aunts. They would shuck corn
or snip peas off the back porch if they could.

Island Vetch

A visitor might admire the genteel wave
of pink clustered blossoms sashaying
down the hill, leaping the double tractor
path to tumble murmuring over the cliff.

"Pretty clover, that," they might say
but even the most polite gardener will
correct, "No, it's Vetch. Not something
to *ever* invite into your garden.

Root systems like capillaries." Panic rises
in her voice. "You can never get rid of them.
Ubiquitous, like bindweed, morning glory
or kudzu—they can bury your house in vines!"

At my chair, I take a bloom, separate one petal,
a miniature sweet pea, yet lavender wing lifts
off a pale cloak, hidden deep within, blue blood
tipped, a curving scimitar, a pirate's seed.

Sea Urchins

The destruction of Byzantium is a daily practice
among herring gulls seizing unsuspecting spiney
urchins off barnacled stones at low tide. Crisp-

winged strokes, red tipped beaks crush and gorge
on delicacies of Japanese sashimi. Gulls hurtle
skyward to litter soft needled paths with shattered

porcelain temples. Fragile spines bleach to lavender,
fade to luminous white. Inside, pointillist lacework
etches a curving architecture built by a soft bellied

hunger. Dawn finds me crouched ankle deep, rubber
sandaled, gazing into a choreography of living spines,
purple filaments swaying in my rippling reflection.

The Old Spruce

Encircled by his past, silvered branches
like antlers protrude from stippled bark,
a stag who never shed a single year's
rack in the mating crash, wreathed in a
lifetime of bone, a skirt of bleached
limbs hanging like swords struck back
into stone. Do these low branches know
they are ancestors of needle-tipped cousins
far above, who grasp light through island
fog? Did this spruce assume greatness from
the start? Not scoffing off childish boughs,
like a painter who stored every sketch, or
a traveler who hoarded each map, the spruce
accumulated an ascending stairway of memory.

In the Summer House Kitchen: Dinner for Artists

Wainscoted walls, top shelf lined with red, black, and gold insignias on tins of tea
Flotilla of knives, ladles, shimmer of grater ridges, measuring cups in a tidy line

Chopping boards etched by a century of knives, stirring spoons, sigh of lids
Ancestors draw close to breathe in stock simmering with scallions, mushrooms

Priests and muses, servants and masters, the cooks snip, toss, test, taste
White hands on black clock inch past 6 p.m.

Bass-voiced cook, Manhattan rich kid in the ancient kitchen becomes great grandson
of Russian Latvian Jews with soul patch, consults Torah for next prayer of butter and salt

Second cook with black curls, straight-backed Persian tenor glances up
Sweet smile above mound of sliced ripe apricots and perfume of strawberries

Bass cook's wrists, a knife dancing duet, anchors red baby potato, slice, quick turn,
quarter, toss into mound, white interiors glisten in lamp light

Scrawled black script: *Grilled Salmon Sauce: 1 shallot and 6 leeks*
Cook till translucent   add wine and sherry vinegar   reduce by 2/3

Bass voice sighs: "15 years ago I had this dish. I've dreamed of it ever since.
Found the recipe from Robuchon. I think this is it!"

Through the open screened window, fog engulfs pine ridges
On rocky shore of islands across the wide channel

Split spruce hisses, sparks in the chrome-gleaming six-burner Queen Atlantic
Steel and enamel caldrons spew clouds rumbling under lids

Melted butter wafts through shrinking mound of shattered shallots and leeks
Wine and sherry hit hot iron, sweet steam

Bass cook talks to the stove: "Don't make me leave you for the propane burner! But I
need some heat! Oh good, caught a major simmer."

Bass: "Oh man, taste the broth!" Voice rises into Julia Child falsetto, "Does this need
a soupçon of salt and white wine? Bon Appetit!" Tenor: "Lovely, lovely. And yes, salt."

Work in 1 tbsp of cream and butter   Garnish with tarragon
Thin sliver cabbage   Blanch in salted water

Fog lifts, hovers above line of spruce silhouettes, gray deepens, cool breeze
Streams through window, waving clothesline of dish cloths, blue-checked, red-striped

From black and white photograph, Josephine, the Swedish cook 80 years ago,
queen of doughnuts and pies, eyes whippersnappers wielding her knives

On the back porch, wringer washer straddles stone sinks, ready to suds and flatten
Iron ready to sear and polish starched high-collared white shirts required at dinner

Sweet grass baskets traded off the dock from the last Wabanakis who fish, feast,
And toss shells onto ancient mound littered with bone hooks and flint arrowheads

Grandmother took her dip on North Beach at dawn. Stained fingers in strawberry
Thickets in South Meadow. Filled her baskets for hand-cranked ice cream

Four door oak panels, brass locking latches on icebox, translucent cubes a boy
Could barely haul, fetched out of packed sawdust from icehouse

Galvanized knee-high bucket, collage of compost, yellow red onion skins, arugula stems.
Depression glass tray, ripe tomatoes sliced red, purple, yellow

White enamel double sink, chrome spigots tightened back
Steaming ribbons of cabbage glow in red pottery platter, toss with butter, salt, pepper

White hands on black clock inch past 7 p.m. Cooks confer, tenor questions bass,
"What's our ETA on grilling the salmon? They're thick!"

Off the back porch, across the reach, fog sinks covering islands, long shadows on water
Flames flicker on grill, licking olive-oiled silver skin on salmon slabs

Steaming potatoes tumble into pottery bowl speckled with parsley butter
Steamed carrots and pea pods slide into green glass bowl

Tenor's fingertips press on sizzling salmon. "If I were a salmon in this heat,
For this length of time, how would I feel?" Tastes hot morsel

Bass voice: "Shit, Shit! A Casualty! Sour dough bread in oven! Oh... saved!"
Rapid sawing, steaming crusted wedges laid on faded green tea towel in wooden bowl

Delicate Persian fingers wield knife like a surgeon, separating salmon into portions
Plate up: delicate cabbage, nestled salmon, savory sauce above and below

Artists carry laden china plates to vast cypress table gleaming in candlelight
Cooks return to kitchen and toss their exuberant arms around each other

For Barney and Nima, Art Week chefs, 2010

Stories from an Island at the Edge of the World

Here we ride in our island lifeboat, cast adrift
from the steady moorings of our days, allowing
stories to drift to the surface. Where the scent
of oils, pastel powder on the thumb, the focusing
of the lens and carving of words sail us out beyond
our known world. Stories turn mythic arising

among strangers on an island. Anina followed
her uncle Eliot as he photographed birds' nests.
She carried them home, lined the walls of her
childhood where she slept for sixty years. The
songbirds so thick, their song so pervasive,
are now so rare. Just the call of gull and crow,

and occasional wren. "It is the silent spring," she says
with grief. Telling of inhabitants of Bear Island across
the reach, Brita tells of the pregnant Margaret Fuller
and her Italian count crossing the North Atlantic in a
storm. When the call went out for women and children
to be saved, she chose to throw her journals in the life raft

and went down with the ship in the arms of her husband.
The next story is of the young and reckless Bucky Fuller
who squandered his inheritance, killed his young daughter
with neglect. He walked into the sea at night, stood up
to his neck, holding the pistol to his head. Staring into
the sky of stars he faced the tragic mystery of his life.

He vowed to learn everything, to understand his life, his
daughter, and why his Aunt chose to slip into the sea. These
tales whisper around the china at the wooden plank table,
past hand-caned chairs and settle, reverberating through
a story I have carried like an old Rookwood vase for fifty
years. At this table, my history shifts perspective.

My great grandmother stood on the deck of the Lucitania
after the crumpling thud of the torpedo, the rapid listing,
the frantic cry. "Women and children to the lifeboats!"
How long did she stand in that brief vast chilling moment
of choice? Survivors reported she was last seen walking arm
and arm with my great grandfather, calmly returning to their

stateroom, leaving my grandmother alone, twenty, at college,
to wake to the news of their vanishing into the North Atlantic.
We sit at the Porters' table of grandparents, uncles and aunts,
Fairfield's paint-spattered easels still on the porch, Eliot's
photographs on the wall, poems to be read next to the fire.
The stories continue. Anina tells of the paths designed

ninety years ago to trace the edges and heights of the island,
the choices made to not cut the woods, to let the trees crash
and rot where they fall, to create soil for the millennia ahead,
rather than cutting, which washes the soil away. It does leave
a tinderbox if there's a fire. "We keep the trees back from the
houses as best we can, but it's a risk we take." The candles are lit.

Bowls of ripe peaches and blueberries are brought to the table.
Rising fog disappears the islands across the reach. In the story
Bucky Fuller headed into a library to read, began with the farthest
reaches of the universe, continued through everything until he
reached the microscopic. He emerged with one word. Integrity.
That is what holds it all together. That was why, he realized, my

aunt made her choice. I suddenly understand. This is why my great
grandmother made her choice. I look around the circle of travelers
who sit at this table at the edge of the world, in the time of the silent
spring, when the vast colony of barn swallows have disappeared from
the island in the last five years. We don't know what we will face, the
call to lifeboats, the choice to slip into the dark sea, the windfall of trees

slowly rotting into soil, the tinderbox. But we each are held together, points around the compass of this table with that one word. Integrity. It is what takes us out into the glean of the meadow grasses to face the day.

With gratitude to the participants in Anina Porter Fuller's Art Week Residency 2005
There are other accounts of Margaret Fuller's death at sea. This is the story I heard.

Inside the Winter Boathouse

The V boarded doors, bolted and impenetrable, hold
storms at bay. The summer's litter of construction, rib
patterns, bolts, knuckle and Y braces blanketed in dust.

Icy tides visit thrice daily, slipping under the open sill,
leaving wrack line offerings, parallel stripes of seaweed,
entwined with burnished orange crab, wave-whittled wood.

Over the long winter, the tarp-cocooned dories, planks taut
as sounding boards, long for the clatter of oars, the galvanized
slip jolt into oarlocks, the certain grasp of work-leathered hands.

The oldest boats languish season after unused season. Forgotten
inside muffled shrouds, the once varnished hulls grow paper
thin and brittle like last year's wasp nests ragged under eaves.

Tug open the door. Can you feel it--the yearning to sail in a
galloping wind, to narrowly miss treacherous ledges, to nuzzle
a star-studded sea in the inhale and exhale of tides all night?

Island Meadow

For days I lay there, drugged amidst the blooming milkweed,
where butterflies rode perfumed thermals for the joy of flight.
I nestled like a deer in the shining grass and could not leave.

While bees foraged in their urgent work, barging with greed
into indolent globes of milky blooms, Victorian pink and white,
for days I lay there, drugged amidst the blooming milkweed.

I stepped through summer's shimmer, orange jolts of hawkweed,
crisp currents of blueberries under foot, sweet fern, knee height.
I nestled like a deer in the shining grass and could not leave.

Mornings in my darkened cabin, I woke to days eclipsed of need,
pillow glancing toward dawn's fingers, streaking golden delight.
For days I lay there, drugged amidst the blooming milkweed.

Butterflies dipped, drank, stroked avalanche of blooms to feed;
a chase, a flutter, a cascade of gauze wings leaping out of sight.
I nestled like a deer in the shining grass and could not leave.

Waking from a dream, happiness flooded, my Beloved held me,
our bodies merged like butterflies, only meadow filled my sight.
For days I lay there, drugged amidst the blooming milkweed.
I nestled like a deer in the shining grass and could not leave.

Where the Beloved Finds Me

The minute I heard my first love story I started looking for you,
not knowing how blind I was. Lovers don't finally meet somewhere.
They're in each other all along. —Rumi

On the fertile shore of a granite island I wake,
flooded with happiness, a sweet sense of being
loved. I rummage through the dream looking for
him. We began by speaking of Requiems, he loves
Fauré. I sleep the sleep of islands, days edged in

granite and spruce. Forests surge with moss, sun-
filled meadows court me, words drift like watercolors
onto wet paper. My mended heart a steady paddle,
dips a path through a quiet evening sea. In the dream,
our bodies touch, wading in cold water at dawn, wave

nuzzled. Eyes closed, body to body, lips to his rich
mouth. *I want to see him!* My eyes open to see no
man, only meadow, fluttering, light-streaked, where
orange butterflies dazzle and tease a cobalt sky. In
the next summer's dream, I turn toward a man's face

but go blind before I see him. He takes my arm, his
fingertips slide back the sleeve of my blouse. It must
be summer to wear a cloth so light. His mouth brushes
across my breast. Startled, desire dazzles, streaking silver
across the bay, yet my arc of vision sees nothing. I only
feel. His lips kiss my sun-burnished skin.

IV. Of Books and Stones:
From a Village in Ohio

A Girl's Fairy Tale

I unfastened the glass bookcase door, reached for
the leather-bound Children's Classics, unopened
for half a century. Sunday's glittering dust floated
upward in the Victorian library when I read, snug
in my rocking chair. Fingering creamy rough-edged
pages, I lingered over Beauty's despair, bereft when
she found her crumpled Beast in the garden. Across
the room, my bald modern father lounged, flicking
glossy pages of architectural magazines, on his black
leather Eames chair and ottoman, polished steel legs
glimmering. Every Sunday he opened a boxed set of
opera records and stacked them on the new stereo.
Two small speakers hurtled a startling radiance into
our silence. My father's voice echoed in fake Italian, his
arms conducted the afternoon. I read fairy tales while I
waited for Mimi's coughs in *La Boheme*, waited the long
terrible pause until her love saw she was dead and sobbed
her name. In the oil portrait over the fireplace, I wore an old-
fashioned dress. My serene smile graced the room, yet I waited
greedily for Aida's scream when she leapt off the palace parapet.

Stones 1959

On a vast smoothed beach on Nantucket, my father
slipped a gray stone into my small hand, "Close your
eyes. Feel the stone." It was cool and buttery smooth.
His voice questioned, "What color is it?" Scrunching

my eyes shut, I worried. How could I feel a color?
All I could 'see' was flashing darkness behind my
eyes. My fingers searched for color on this smooth
disc the sea slid across a sandpaper beach all day.

My mind's eye filled with a sunset. Brilliant oily pastels
on textured paper I'd drawn the night before. I gasped,
"It's bright red with orange streaks!" Behind his black-
framed glasses, his eyes beamed approval into mine.

Running into the salty wind, hair whipped my face,
I scanned the burnished beach to find my own stone.
I took his hand. "Close your eyes." My voice urgent.
"Tell me the color you feel." His wide thumb moved

in a small circle over the stone. My dad in his Mexican
shirt with carved bone buttons, kneeling, his sunburned
bald head even with mine, he opened his gray-blue eyes.
"It's Navajo turquoise with a streak of silver in the groove."

I nodded, smiling into his intense eyes. Oh, my Daddy,
I felt more alive with him than with anyone else.

Writing My Name Inside of Books

How old was I the Saturday morning I sobbed
over the death of Laura's old dog Jack, the day
they moved west toward the remaining "Little
House" books on the shelf over my head?

Was that the day I wrote my full name with a ·
thick pencil, large cursive letters, even my
long middle name, taking up half the page, as
I jealously claimed each book for myself?

Some books I never wrote in, hand-me-down
Nancy Drews I read with embarrassed fervor,
but my teenage signature sprawled proudly
across the blank front pages of the Brontes.

College-tattered Lattimore's *Odyssey*, my
reading history crammed into years:'74 UC;
'74 Hopkins; '75 Harvard;'76 Hopkins. Earnest
notes: *The problem of heroes without war. The*

importance of marrying Penelope. Late twenties,
passionate underlining of Christian mystics, my·
name graceful, followed by *April '82. On second
day alone, lying in meadow at Pt Reyes, walking*

on the plains of God's heart. A tuft of wild grasses,
yellowed seed pods fall. Pages inscribed *with love*
to old boyfriends still carry desire, *I can't wait
to stay up late, reading poems that move us to awe.*

I gave my father my underlined copy of Jung's *Memories,
Dreams and Reflections*, hoping if I gave him my most
precious books, he would be saved from his lost years.
But he left them behind and they washed away in a desert

flood. Rilke's poems, spine split over twenty years, my name
is followed by my baby son's jealous scribble in blue marker,
staking his claim to my private life.
                                    Now I don't leave any
name, like grasses righting after footsteps cross a meadow.

Our Mothers

It was always hot those summers in the fifties,
when my aunt in New York City and my mother
in a village in Ohio sent postcards saying, *Finally
got the kids to bed. Just mopped the kitchen floor.
I'm having a smoke and writing to you before I go
to sleep. Will see you at the farm, soon! Love, Me*

We helped our sweating mothers pack VW buses,
make deviled eggs, put blocks of ice in coolers.
Homemade bread sandwiches crumbling in waxed
paper bags. Our fathers left behind as our mothers
set out toward the farm of their childhood. Their
cars, like two arrows, moved across the map toward

Buffalo, following state route numbers through small
towns, speed traps, stop signs, off ramps, construction.
New highways slowly made a long unbroken path
between where we lived and our grandmother's house.
Cars steamed with panting dogs, wet diapers, crumbs,
new baby crying, big kids helpful, playing one more

round of Go Fish before asking, *Are we almost there?*
When we reached the first field of the farm, excitement
shivered through us as we passed the lower fields, barns,
the back drive through pine windbreak, before turning
off the road at the great oak at the long front drive. Our
cars slipped past a parade of peonies, their extravagant

blossoms collapsed into grass, crawling with ants. At the
gray clapboarded farmhouse sheltered under maples, we
tumbled out of cars into our grandmother's arms and the
golden afternoon. If we had turned to watch our mothers
stepping into their mother's world of the table set, earthen-
ware cookie jar full, dinner warm in the oven, beds made

with fresh-smelling sheets, we would have seen the weight
lift off their shoulders, seen them turn into girls, like baby
sitters in seersucker shorts. We floated past them, happy in
our life raft of cousins, mornings in the sandbox, lunch on
picnic blankets, naps on the sleeping porch, where we watched
our mothers run laughing to the pond, like girls, our mothers.

Bossy Girl

It was the peak of my fifth grade writing year, the Thanksgiving play
    at grandmother's farm with my cousins
and brothers ready to costume and direct. I gathered my motley
    cast in the library: Bunny, with short skinny
pigtails, Keek, scrawny in his crewcut, Tigger, commanding in her
    long braids, watching over her little brothers,
and mine: Hubbard, his broken arm in a sling, and my faithful little
    Woodie wearing his favorite black velvet cape
and carrying a little wooden sword. Inspired by history, surrounded by
    shelves of leather books so soft and old they
left streaks on your fingers, I informed them my newest play was about
    Sarah Josepha Hale, editor of Godey's Lady's
Book, whose editorials pressured President Lincoln into proclaiming
    Thanksgiving a holiday in 1863. I had pages
of dialogue leading to the climax of her meeting with Lincoln, drawings
    of costumes, and Grandmother said, "if
we were very careful, we could use grandfather's satin top hat that popped
    up if you punched it in the middle." Puffed
with pride, filled with urgency, I ended importantly, "And all the grown-ups
    want to see the play!" The rebellion began
slowly, but complete mutiny was swift. I was left watching their scrawny
    backs in striped tee shirts, little legs in jeans,
scuffed shoes jostling past the piano, shoving out the front door, cheers
    of liberation as they ran round the circle
drive heading for the straw fort in the barns. I ran to the kitchen. My glasses
    steamed, my mother basted the enormous
turkey, aunts rolled pie crust, Grandmother washed brussels sprouts from
    the garden, and I lamented, "They won't be
in my play! I'm ruined!" Unsympathetically, my mother said, "You can't
    make people do what they don't want to do."

Where does the bossy girl live now, decades later? When my love started
    quietly to pull away, all I knew was that I
was scared, but a wanting, a grasping, a pressuring began so the plan
    would still unfold, so the cast would follow
the script, only, once again, a kind of mutiny.... As I walked away
    that last snowy day, looking back, I saw
him standing in the doorway, peering out like a scared little boy
    in a striped shirt, bashful, yet relieved,
to have escaped the play a bossy girl had scripted and tried to direct.

A Private History of Cocks

i. my daddy

my daddy said
it's good to be naked
walking round the house
wrinkled butt
free as a bird

puts his TIME magazine
in front of himself
when he answers the door
when my friends come
to visit

my daddy said he's not Victorian
not going to have us grow up
not knowing anything
never seeing anyone naked
not knowing anything about
sex

here let me teach you

he's naked on his bed
with that wrinkled
gray
animal
in his lap
all hairy
and crooked
trail of slime on his leg
like slugs
in the garden

puts his finger in
that slime trail
puts it on my fingers
this is lubrication
this is how you'll have
sex

ii. first boyfriend

I could have kissed
forever
kept everything up
close to our eyes
our mouths
kissing and talking
forever

but this yearning
sinking
dissolving
gravity
kept pulling
us down

but we'd get near that place
and I'd start trembling
shaking
months of shaking
before I could even
touch
you

slowly we
uncovered
you
were so
beautiful

like sculpture,
carved
ebony
rising from
your fur
your thighs

I, like cream,
poured into
your arms

iii. father of my children

so many years
he held me
just held me

but, in the dark
his good hands
kept turning
into my father's hands

I couldn't bear
that touch

we curled
like spoons
breathing
safety
for years

it takes so long
to heal

is there time enough
in the world
to heal
all the harm
done

iv. my boy

my brown-eyed baby boy
delicate little stamen
in the blossom of his golden thighs

so afraid, at first,
I'd hurt him
do something
wrong

but months of diapers
wiping poop
out of every
crevice
laughing at pee
fountain

he loved that thing
that rubbery hard/soft tail
of himself
to grab onto
as he ran naked
holding onto his little steed
stretching
pulling himself
as he ran

when my mother said
> *that's enough, you're going to wear*
> *that little thing out*

he ran off laughing,
> holding onto his good thing

Inspired by poet June Jordan's courage

Dancing School

Worn white gloves, scalloped at my wrists, and the repetitive
    beat of the Cha Cha Cha,
punctuated politely by patent leather shoes, carry me back
    to Madame Federova's dancing
school in 1965, when I had to pee so badly but I couldn't bear
    the shame of being seen leaving
a dance to pass the couples crowding the gleaming ballroom
    floor to reach the powder room.
We were the white seventh grade boys and girls of Cincinnati,
    selected from the Blue Book,
carpooled by parents from the nice neighborhoods, carloads
    beelining over city parkways
for the hotel's weary entrance, wrought iron lace, cantilevered
    rows of lights shining on the tuxedoed
black doorman, opening car doors, the explosion of polished shoes
    running up the steps, across the maroon
velvety carpet to the Ballroom, where Madame's German accent
    commanded us: *Form two circles.*
Girls facing boys. Take your positions for Fox Trot.

Our lives were littered with minefields: underwear, periods and their
    specialized equipment, stockings
and garter belts, sweat stains under raised armpits, razor-cut shaved
    legs, and the oldest of them all, peeing.
You prided yourself on not having to go all day at school,
    no walk down echoing hallways
with all eyes on you as you passed the open classroom doors.
    How did we become so trained
in our private mortifications and so blind to the obvious?
    How were we taught to not notice
what was right in front of us, so much so that a girl in a dancing
    school, would let the agony of embarrassment
reach such a pitch until pee streaked down her legs, staining
    white ankle socks?
Still it streamed, but she and the nice boy noticed nothing,
    concentrating on
one-two-cha-cha-cha, turn, return, dancing away from the puddle.

In the rain-streaked night, carpools drove us home out of the city,
    traffic lights smearing
ruby across wet asphalt, white children's faces, pale ghostly
    moons gazing out of car windows
wound up tight. White mothers' faces taut, at the wheel, like that
    mother of five, homemaker from Detroit,
it says in the paper, driving a carpool like this one, filled with
    tired black marchers going home to Selma:
when a car pulled alongside, four white men, window wound down,
    barrel pointed, two shots in the head, into
a mother's head driving a car like this one. We are tired, lulled in
    our dark carpool, the thrum-thrum-thrum
of the windshield wipers. One girl says, it was so weird, there was
    a big puddle on the floor and I fell into it
but no one says anything, as we watch constellations in the windows
    of brick apartment buildings, glittering
neon of late night liquor stores on the corner, lingering black men
    gesturing and street talking. A deep voice
calls out, piercing our rain-streaked windows, laughing "You don't
    know nothin', you sorry-ass honky."

His Lips

Not that I'm racist, my father lectured. *But
I never want the two of you out as a couple,
only in odd numbered groups.* How we rolled
our eyes, Alvin and I, seventeen in Ohio 1970.
Alvin's mom was cool, fussing over us, teasing
our starry-eyed looks. She'd turn sternly to his
younger brother, *Hold that lip in before I knock
it in. Don't want anyone thinking you're a dumb
nigger.* I'd never heard that word said out loud.
Alvin laughed, *I learned to keep my lips tucked in.*

We'd become friends in Trigonometry, struggling
over sines and cosines, my pale winter fingers
traced out waves on grids. Busty white girls
in angora passed him notes. *"I'm lusting after
your body. Want to meet after school?"* His brown
cheeks blushed darker. We grew closer in English,
speed-reading Drieser's *American Tragedy.* I crowed,
I got to page 580! He grinned. *Sorry kiddo, I'm at 614!*

I was the Twiggy skinny girl with no bra, tortoise
shell glasses, and he melted: *I never thought I'd
find anyone I could talk to about the Tibetan Book
of the Dead.* We were the first born of famous fathers:
his – first African American state legislator, mine –
designing sixties modern buildings in the city. He
erased his black accent to sound white. I erased
any trace of Ohio twang. We both wanted to sound
not from here. We fell in love talking.

First kiss at our first rock concert, deafened by *Ten
Years After,* we dissolved into heart-pounding softness.
Then everything got complicated. I opened my eyes,
saw people scowling, staring, turning away. I'd crossed
a line, disappearing into the delicious pillows of his lips.

At school, black girls turned away muttering, *You stay away from our men.* We learned to hide. My empty house after school, or his. Kissing was our world. Desire moved our hands lower, but I shook for hours, terrified. Weekends, my father interrogated: *Have you lost your virginity? Answer me! I'm going to pull you out of school and end this relationship.*

Senior year, everyone wearing black antiwar armbands on Moratorium Day was rounded up, held in the auditorium. Protest rallies spilled out of Fountain Square, edged with police in riot gear. We held onto each other. In gymnastics, he leapt, swung, catapulted, and on the hanging rings he stretched out into the Iron cross, my smart hero. We applied to colleges. I was going east, he to Ann Arbor. We planned our futures and cried. I secretly dreamed of our babies. Little realizing how easily I would leave at the end of summer, slipping back under the cloak of whiteness.

At the state finals, he came in second, falling near the end, splitting his upper lip. Celebrating with an icepack, his pink inner lips blossomed like a camellia. Embarrassed, I went home early, waiting for the swelling to go down, waiting for him to look smart again, like someone I would be seen with.

Coins in My Father's Pocket

that nervous rattle
quarters, dimes, and nickels
dashing against his worn pocket-knife
clattering among his lonely keys
his trembling hand in his khaki pocket
comforting his grief in the tangle of metal
constant movement against weakening legs
that distracted, frustrated, saddened me

and he didn't even notice he made a sound

Stones 1994

Off the coast of Maine, there are double beaches
where waves forever tumble black stones in deep
water, shifting, rolling off Brimstone Island. Never
a certain place to anchor, in any kind of wind.

I've met people who carry small Brimstones
in their pockets for years, oiled by dirt
and loose change, the stone fitting the pinch
of their fingers, a quiet pleasure.

One of my acupuncture patients brought me one
that fit perfectly, like a child's hand in my palm.
Patients who were afraid of the brief needle sting
held the stone for comfort. When my father died,

as I packed and dashed before dawn for my flight,
I took the black stone in my pocket. That last day
he lay in the weight of the world, his body covered
in gray cloth, I uncovered his heavy hand, curled

into a fist. My hands warmed his cold clenched
fingers, working the black sea-smoothed Brimstone
until it disappeared into his grasp, so he would not be
alone when he slipped into the blue-laced orange fire.

Critique

Arlene speaks to me across the table of writers discussing my story. *You're talking about the black woman who cared for you when you were a little girl like she's some old Aunt Jemima. How you loved her. How good she was to you. But she was an employee. She was doing her job. Did you know anything about her?* My cheeks, eyes

burn. I want to say you don't understand. She cared about me. I was her special little girl. It wasn't just a job. Arlene speaks carefully. *It sounds like she was doing a really good job. But she didn't love you. She was being paid.* She pauses, looks down before she lifts her eyes, weary and wet. *You are writing about my mother.*

She looked like Aunt Jemima. When she came home she was worn out. Didn't have anything left for us. We are both in our fifties, no make-up, hair graying, hers braided close to her head, mine short and wavy, both in tears. Arlene continues. *Don't you see, when you went to see her as an old woman, you still wanted her to take care*

of you. But you knew that, that's why you wrote that the people on the street were saying, 'what you doing here, white lady?' Arlene is right. I still wanted her warm voice to curl around me like it did when I was a girl, saying 'Oh, chile, everythin's gonna be alright.' Still wanting even when she was an old woman, crippled with

arthritis, on her porch swing with her great-grandchildren on the black side of town. Arlene continues. *I don't understand what you mean about missing the sound of how we talk? Black vernacular is everywhere. Why don't you turn on the television!* I try to explain. *I live in Maine, the whitest state in the country. I don't even own a*

television. I miss the languages of my childhood. She looks at me a long time. *I didn't know anyone lived in such a homogeneous place.* She glances down at her notes. *In your poem where your dad says 'I'm not a racist, but I never want you out as a couple, only in odd-numbered groups.' That sounds like how I was with my kids. I was on them all the time. Be careful, don't trust those white people.* I look at her amazed. I thought only white people said things like that. At lunch, she puts her arm around me, introduces me as her new friend. Later she looks me over, pronounces, *"Girl, you got some hips on you!"* We laugh.

Last Kiss

When [black men] learn that death is as near as a shadow and go about living their lives accordingly...they become more beautiful than even God could imagine. —Edward P. Jones

first love   forbidden angel   40 years   later

meet for breakfast   eyes falter   glance

    smile   *what was*   *our song?*

("white bird in a golden cage")

close-cut gray   burnished chestnut skull   *I'm diminishing*

points to chemo pill

    don't even touch it

    everything changes when
    you're terminal

("play your love song all night long")

dumbfounded tears   crushed in a leather jacket

glances sweep   catch   in mustache

remember   upsweep   of lips

    when I memorized them   for hours

your father didn't separate us
    we made it

everything changes

    when you're terminal

("in a white room with black curtains")

our whole life is preparation   *for death*

slide by   undiminished eyes

    precarious

can't look   too long   into a (happily) married
man's eyes

                  linger   search   gaze

                  when the inevitable   comes calling

   I'm making a video   *(I'm a geek,*   *I*   *confess)*

     drain water   lick lips   linger
                         ("a long long time before the dawn")

eyes quicken   grasp on
                    eyes   release   scatter

   everything changes
              chaste whisper of lips
                      (when you're terminal)

Physics Lesson

My heart has left its dwelling place
and can return no more. —John Clare

        narrow bridge towers over Maine river
        procession of cars
        when road opens out

sudden invisible quiet   in my chest   pause (no beat) pause (no beat)

        view of grayed pavement thins
        dulled curves of windshield

    fade to   pale

less   than   a second   to pull right

      before fainting   into blind   emptiness

      *   *   *

Tall skinny boy in grade school, he captained ancients
versus moderns in the debate, "Is the world flat or round."
Because he introduced epicycles to explain retrograde
motion (this was just fourth grade), his team won. He went
to Princeton, became a physics professor until a brain
aneurysm in his forties left him propped in a wheelchair.
He concentrates a floundering hand to press his index
finger through a guide that allows him to type one letter
at a time, in a perfectly executed row, then presses Send.

> *The physics Nobel prize... honors the astronomers who discovered that the*
> *expansion of the universe is speeding up, not slowing down, as was universally*
> *assumed before.*

      *   *   *

My first love (slowly dying) emails from Minnesota prairie:

That's so weird. Two days ago, I passed out too, in the kitchen. I wasn't out more than a
couple of seconds, and didn't injure myself falling. My wife was out of town all week and
our dog was being a shit. He would not come in and in fact spent the night outside. The
next day, I ended up in the ER and in overnight. Hey, we can be heart patient pals!

*   *   *

sightless   with   out   body

as if   time   wavered   I   disappeared   falling

          thud   *where am I*

                              was that   *my tire?*

thud   *have I stopped*

                                        am I   *in the road*

          foot holds brake   even though   I   vanish
                                                                       for a moment

*   *   *

Brain imploded, blood billowed through
delicate folds and soft chambers. Body
droops yet his mind still lasers into words,
finger types one agonizing letter at a time

> *The key here is how they determined how far away distant galaxies are.... Since all Type 1a supernovae have the same absolute brightness, the observed brightness tells you the distance...Using the constant speed of light, a red shift-distance relation becomes a red shift-time relation. From this they see that nearby (recent) galaxies are receding faster than distant (ancient) ones. That tells you that the expansion of the universe is accelerating.*

*   *   *

On the phone from Minnesota, he puzzles,

This happened two summers ago, don't you remember? I found myself on the floor and forty minutes had gone by. The dog was licking my face and I kept staring at my watch. Next day you told me on the phone, "That's so weird," because two days before, you were sitting on a beach and keeled over. After a dip in freezing saltwater. You won't get me to swim in water that cold! You came to on your side in the sand, arms scrambling to push yourself back up.

```
        *                    *                    *

Route One          ordinary   day              unperturbed   light

        denies any            disappearance
                                     engine purrs
patiently

except            car is tilted              straddles          sidewalk

      could have
              might have    (thank god      only going      25 miles   an
hour)


              didn't


        *                    *                    *
```

At dancing school in seventh grade, I wanted
to dance with him, tall awkward boy with dark
eyes. When my daughter asked for stories of my
childhood, I included the shy boy who didn't ask
me to dance. Now he's the physicist who sends
science articles from his nursing home newsletter.

> It's as if some otherwise unknown repulsive force is pushing galaxies apart more than
> gravity is pulling them together. If it increases, the universe could end with the "big
> rip," where this new repulsion eventually dominates over all attractive forces, and
> everything flies apart. At the other extreme, the new force declines and becomes negli-
> gible. Which scenario we will get is yet unknown. Stay tuned.


```
        *                    *                    *
```

First love, we vowed (at 17): We Love Each Other.
He gave me his gymnastics medal. I gave him my
National Honor Society medal. We etched our secret
code, WLEO, on the back. His medal still in my desk.

```
        *                    *                    *
```

He ends his email,
              It's strange,
                    as if our hearts are still tied.

Stones 2007

I brought my new love stones from Herring
Cove in a bowl of water. My first gift. They
slipped, agate red, jasper green, speckled
granite, between our fingers, as we spoke

of stones. I told him, "After my father died,
I took one of the black smooth stones from
Brimstone Island and pressed it into his hand."
He gazed at me, "After my wife died, I filled

her hands with stones from Brimstone Island."
We looked at each other a long time, before
turning away. Later he wondered out loud,
 "Who are you to be in my life?"

He wept when I wrote "I want to have
loved someone so much, that they would
fill my hands with stones when I leave.
I would offer that gift to them."

                *   *

A year later, after he said we were over,
he confessed, "I didn't love you enough
to fill your hands with stones when you
died." Later, after he closed the door and

I drove away, I knew I could love anyone
well enough to leave a stone in their hands.

V. Down East Journey: In Memoriam

Down East Journey: In Memoriam

For twenty years, Tuffy had been stopping by our homestead on a hill in Brooks. Down from Pleasant Point she arrived with fresh braided sweet-grass from up north in late summer, fiddleheads from the western mountains in the spring, spruce wreath from the mountains in winter, and every fall her newest moose hunting story. We ate our fill of fresh moose and fry bread, laughing harder than we'd ever laughed, silly on moose meat, the way we always laughed when Tuffy came visiting, calling her our grandmi.

I was overwhelmed with children and gardens. Tuffy washed my sink of dishes and made cornbread. We thanked the food. Tuffy spoke each name aloud in Passamaquoddy, to honor potatoes, beans, bread, meat. As we canned dilly beans or peaches, froze corn or applesauce, she told stories of the women battling against the gambling casino, meeting with legislators in Augusta, their holy war, fighting for the soul of their people.

It's been years now. Children nearly grown, Tuffy still visits since I moved to town, but she's been slowing down. This January thaw, a strange fifty degrees warm and melting, it's my turn to load up the car, with a farmer friend's good onions, winter squash, healthy chicken, and badatos, as Tuffy calls potatoes, for me to visit her "up to Pleasant Point."

Heading north on Route One, the first hour I pass all that's familiar. After Ellsworth, the landscape goes wilder. Glacier scraped soil, shorter trees, blueberry barrens. Towns shrink leaner, Hancock, Sullivan, Steuben, wearied under a heavy gray sky. Follow signs through sprays of rain on a worn windshield, another hour, Millbridge, Columbia Falls, Machias. Another hour and still not there. Route 1 becomes a narrow worn track through forests. Logging trucks barrel by in spray of sea squalls. Up the coast, flags at half-mast honor the Passamaquoddy Tribal Governor who died on a road near here two days before, sleep or black ice careening his pickup across a bridge before he hit the oil truck.

The settlement of Pleasant Point follows a narrow spit of land surrounded by the storm's high tide. I turn on the last road, pass the Catholic Church, park on Elder's Way, and find Tuffy's door. She calls me in. Waking from a nap, bright eyes, cheeks smooth and flushed from sleep, she laughs to see me, while the sea roils and leaps a stone's throw from her window.

"Isn't it a joke to think I'm here in Elderly housing, when I don't feel a day over thirty. Will you look at this, electricity and running water, when I've been living in that cabin at Alder Stream for the last twenty years. Can you believe it, your Gabe was a baby crawling around in a garbage bag for a raincoat when we were all building it! But I'm loving having a rest after all that work. I'm so happy to be home again."

"After the first day of that chemo, I said, enough of that! I wrote to all my friends for help. I knew in a week, I'd start hearing back. I've got my Essiac tea simmering, and Deanna taught me T'ai Chi that I do every morning. I look out at the ocean. Oh, it's just so beautiful here. I draw up all the bad and move it up and out of me, over and over, until it's all gone. Then I bring in the good, wave it in off the ocean, and fill myself up with it."

I cook our lunch in her kitchen, and she settles into a recliner. Out the window the hearse leaves the community center next door, leaving the coffin of their chief for a two day wake. The people are bringing trays of food and flowers. On the beach there is a fire burning night and day, despite the wind and this strange warm rain, until his funeral in four days when Maine Governor Baldacci will come to pay his respects.

"The last nun at the church came by and asked if I wanted Communion. I said, "No thank you, dear." She said, "Well, if you change your mind, just let me know." She thinks that my getting sick is going to make me suddenly change my mind! I don't think so!"

The ladies come to visit Tuffy. Their words sew seamlessly back and forth between Passamaquoddy and English. Deanna, the Osteopath, went to school off and on for thirty years to become the first woman doctor from the Reserve. Tall and handsome, long black braid down her back, Native Health Services from Detroit flies her out to work a week out of every month. "It's in the Hood," she says, "with drive-by shootings. They break in the clinic about three times a year and steal the computers. But that week pays me enough to have three weeks here where I treat whoever needs me."

She brings Tuffy mussels she gathered. "Strengthening and cleansing," she says, "good medicine." They talk of the old man, Dickie, so frail, she visits him daily. "Couldn't get to him until ll:30 last night. He said, 'I thought you'd forgotten me.'" She answered. "I promised I'd be here. He hasn't eaten." They all count. "It's 38 days now, just a little water. He's waiting to rejoin his Dee. She visited him in his dream the other night." She tells us what Carol, the Tribal Chief's wife, said just last Saturday. He'd told her when I die, I want to be cremated, and I want to be dressed with the special sash. They all nod. "Spirit was already calling him."

A broad shouldered man appears at the door telling Deanna they have nine fresh killed rabbits for her. Tuffy tells her how to skin and gut them. "It's good if you have two nails on the outside of your house. You attach the fur at the feet and pull hard. It all comes off, turning inside out."

Bonnie arrives beaming with energy. She puts in her forty hours at the place they sew camouflage pants with lead in them to protect soldiers against explosions. She was so pleased when they asked her to work up at the Wabanaki Store. "Another twenty hours. It's good. That's when I get my visiting in."

So many people get laid off in the winter. But they agree, you can always find some work if you try. Even if it's "wrinkling." Why even Andrea, the one handed woman. She was born that way, the other arm, a little withered stump she'd hit people with. She hauls her sled along the beach, and lifts the sea weed to find periwinkles. Picks them so fast, faster than anybody. She can fill a whole onion bag in a day and makes $90 for it. Bonnie says, "They send them to China where they are some kind of delicacy. I bet they pay a lot of money for them there."

Tuffy says, "When we were kids, we'd pick them. We'd fill an old can with some sea water, put seaweed on top and build a little fire. Just down there on the beach we cooked them up. You needed a safety pin or a bobby pin to open the shell and pull out the little worm. Oh, they were so good!"

They talk of the people who married out, and left the reservation thirty years ago. They count, if he's first cousin, then they must be second and third cousins. Tuffy's name is Georgia Mitchell, related to the Francis family, related to everyone. They speak of the fear of driving at night, not driving after 3:30pm when the roads ice over. After they leave, it's way past four when I've given Tuffy her acupuncture treatment. She smiles. "I feel so good, all smoothed out." I assure her that I'll get home safe. "See how warm the wind still is. Have to get home before snow comes in the morning."

She brings me a tall-handled, brown ash woven basket. "This morning I went down to Peter Neptune's and looked at his baskets. I said, 'I have to have something special.' I saw this and knew it was just right for you to carry your things when you go to treat people. I wanted you to have a basket made by a master. I put in a braid of sweet grass." We hug again and again.

I head south in the early dark. Driving rain, hours steering a path between forests. Towns glance by in a scattering of light. Up on ridges, wind from the ocean dumps rain so thick I can't see the road. Cars travel slowly in packs. My ears grasp onto every note on Saturday night public radio to hold me awake.

Finally I reach my little town, where cars cluster around the movie theater, traffic light at the center of town swings in the gale, red light sheens out over wet streets. In the morning, trees and roads are ice coated, 12 degrees and dropping. January thaw is over.

In Memoriam
Georgia Mitchell 2006
Deanna Mae Francis, D.O. 2010

... and left nothing but tender affection. —Jane Austen

About the Poet:

Elizabeth Garber grew up in a village in Ohio. After leaving home, she lived on a square-rigged sailing ship, searched for buildings by Le Corbusier in France, studied Greek epic and Mythology at Harvard and Johns Hopkins, and worked as a carpenter in Berkeley, CA. She studied Five Element Acupuncture which she has practiced in Belfast, Maine for nearly thirty years. She is the mother of two young adults, and lives and gardens near Penobscot Bay.

The 2006 Poet Laureate of Belfast, Maine, she is the author of two books of poetry, *Listening Inside the Dance* (2005) and *Pierced by the Seasons* (2004.) Three of her poems have been read by Garrison Keillor on The Writer's Almanac and "Feasting" was included in his *Good Poems for Hard Times*.

As 2006 Poet Laureate of Belfast, she coordinated monthly poetry readings, and wrote a weekly poetry column published in three mid-coast newspapers highlighting Maine poets. She is the founder of The Illuminated Sea Press, encouraging the independent publishing of fine Maine poets. She was one of the original organizers of the Belfast Poetry Festival and initiated The Poetry and Art Walk, encouraging the collaboration of artists and poets. An hour-long community television program, a Visit with Poet Laureate Elizabeth Garber can be seen http://vimeo.com/12794988.

Elizabeth is collaborating with painter/photographer Michael Weymouth on *MAINE: A SHARED VIEW.* http://mainesharedview.tumblr.com/

Elizabeth is completing two memoirs *The Architect's Daughter* and *A Last Great Love.* Her prologue, "Stones," won the Maine Writer's and Publishers Alliance 2009 Literary Award for unpublished Non-Fiction. She received an MFA from Stonecoast at the University of Southern Maine. She was awarded two writing fellowships in 2010, at Virginia Center for Creative Arts and Jentel Artist Residency Program in Wyoming. Her conversation with Maine poet Dawn Potter entitled "Poets Writing Memoir" is available as a podcast from the Maine Humanities Council. http://mainehumanities.org/podcast/archives/category/literature/memoir

Her website is www.elizabethgarberpoetry.com.

Acknowledgements:

With profound gratitude to my poet mentors who have rigorously challenged and encouraged me for years: Kate Barnes, Gray Jacobik, and Baron Wormser, as well as brief important work with Candice Stover and Arielle Greenberg. I am thankful to have been part of the intense alchemy I experienced in the Stonecoast MFA program at the University of Southern Maine, and especially the Writing about Race seminar with Tim Seibles, Richard Hoffman, Patricia Smith, and my classmates.

With deep appreciation to my poetry and prose writing buddy, Linda Buckmaster, for our years of commitment to writing, reading, editing, and support.

With thankfulness for my readers who have responded generously for decades: Gabriel and Miriam Baldwin, Louise Bourne, Diane Brott Courant, Martha Derbyshire, Elizabeth IlgenFritz, Alvin McClure, Alexandra Merrill, Lauren Murray, and Vicki Pollard.

I have been inspired by the generous opportunity to return for many years to Great Spruce Head Island during Anina Porter Fuller's Art Week and to work in collaboration with painter/photographer Michael Weymouth.

With thanks to my production team: Catlin Barnes, Gretchen Warsen, and Ed Miller.